MW01070770

HACHIKO

THE TRUE STORY OF
THE ROYAL DOGS OF JAPAN
AND ONE FAITHFUL AKITA

HACHIKO

THE TRUE STORY OF
THE ROYAL DOGS OF JAPAN
AND ONE FAITHFUL AKITA

BY JULIE CHRYSTYN

DOVE
BOOKS

ISBN-10: 1-59777-629-7
ISBN-13: 978-1-59777-629-5
Library of Congress Cataloging-In-Publication Data Available

Creative development by Rocky Hill Group, Inc. and JudyO Productions, Inc.
Cover Design by Sonia Fiore
Cover Photo by Sarah K. Chen Photography
Wikimedia Commons: page 7, page 14, page 21: Lombroso (accessed January 8, 2009. Permission granted under
the terms of the GNU Free Documentation License. http://creativecommons.org/licenses/by-sa/2.5/)
Galina Shapareva-Deloof-Sys, www.akita-hachimantai.com: page 8, page 9
Photo courtesy of the National Museum of Nature and Science, Japan: page 22
Akita Photographs courtesy of Suki Mahar, Aoyama Japanese Dogs: Kumori page 11, page 26, page 29, page 39
Courtesy of the American Foundation for the Blind, Helen Keller Archives: page 34
Photo by Booth Photography, courtesy of Marci Howard: Devpoints - CH TimberSky TopSecret Shiojiri owned
by Marcie Howard, bred by Jodi Lundin and Colleen Sullivan, page 37
Photos by Kaitlyn Makenzie Pearce: Zabi, page 41; Maggie, page 49; Lola and Maggie, page 50
Courtesy of Marci Howard: page 44
Courtesy of Tinny Abogado: page 42, page 47

Illustrations by Priscilla Burris: page 10, page 28, page 29

Printed in the United States of America

Dove Books, Inc.
9465 Wilshire Boulevard, Suite 840
Beverly Hills, CA 90212

10 9 8 7 6 5 4 3 2 1

1 0 4 2 0 1 0

PART ONE
THE STORY OF HACHIKO

Hachiko in later life.

On a chilly autumn morning in the hill country of northern Japan, a tiny, cream-white puppy snuggled close to his mother's warm fur. The little dog would one day become a legend beloved by millions. At the moment he was happy just to sleep in a cozy cottage with his brothers and sisters.

The gentle puppy was born on November 10, 1923, in Odate, a peaceful castle town near the northern border of an area called Akita. It was a mountainous realm. Summer rains fed streams that flowed through forests of maple and cedar. When winter brought freezing winds, snow blanketed the landscape. The puppy belonged to a breed of dogs that shared the name of the rugged land. He was an Akita. He would grow up strong and sure-footed, with a thick double coat of soft fur that was almost weatherproof.

Near Hachiko's birthplace in Odate, Japan.

The house where Hachiko was born in Odate, Japan.

At the age of eight weeks, the puppy was just old enough to leave his canine family. His temporary guardian tucked him safely in a traveling basket lined with straw. Together they began a long journey to his new home in the Shibuya district of Tokyo.

He would belong to Professor Eizaburo Ueno. The professor was a member of the Agricultural Department at the Imperial Tokyo University. The puppy was a gift to the professor from one of his students.

It's a Fact: Puppies should remain with their mother until at least eight weeks of age. Twelve weeks is even better because the young dogs learn important lessons from their canine family.

Professor Ueno was a kind, well-respected man in his fifties. He had always been a dog lover and looked forward to meeting his new friend. He bonded with the sweet-faced pup as soon as he saw

him. The professor had chosen a fine name. He called the little dog Hachi. Hachi is Japanese for the number eight, which stands for confidence. It is also thought to bring good fortune. Eventually the name became Hachiko. In the Japanese culture, the "ko" ending is often used for a child. It is also considered a term of respect.

Professor Eizaburo Ueno.

It's a Fact: Professor Eizaburo Ueno was an important Japanese scientist. He is known as the founder of modern irrigation and drainage practices in farming.

Hachiko would probably have liked to spend every moment with his master, but the professor passed his days at the university. On most mornings, Ueno took the train to work. Sometimes he commuted to the agricultural department in Komaba. Sometimes he traveled to the agricultural experimental station in Nishihara. He always left from Shibuya Station. It didn't take long for Hachiko to learn the routine. Dog and master walked to the train station in the morning.

The routine was always the same. The professor would pat Hachiko gently on the head and tell him to be a good boy. With one last wave he would slip through the gate to the platform. As much as he may have wanted to, Hachiko was not allowed to follow. Sometimes he returned home at once. When the weather was nice he probably took his time,

Hachiko may have looked like this puppy when he was young.

sniffing and exploring along the way. As the sun dipped toward the horizon, Hachiko knew his beloved master would soon return to the station, and he would trot off to meet him there.

In the 1920s Shibuya was a small community. The neighborhood near the train station was lined with family-owned shops. The shopkeepers knew each other and most of the daily travelers well. The entrance was never crowded, and Hachiko was able to sit comfortably with a good view of the arriving passengers. He would wait by the ticket booth until he could see Ueno's smiling face. As the professor walked through the gate, Hachiko would wag his tail in a happy greeting.

As the weeks passed Hachiko grew into a fine Akita. The graceful dog was about two feet tall and weighed ninety pounds. His lush, thick fur gleamed in the sun. He held his curled tail high and to the left. Hachiko's love for Professor Ueno grew too. In Japan, Akitas are sometimes described as "ikken isshu," or one-person dogs. Hachiko's one special person was the professor. It seemed that life was perfect when the two were together.

On May 21, 1925, the day began as usual. The soft pink and white cherry blossoms of spring had fallen. The trees were bursting with tender green leaves. Hachiko and the professor walked briskly to the station. The dog sat dutifully as Ueno gave him a loving pat on the head. Late in the afternoon the Akita was back in the same spot. He searched for his master among the stream of returning passengers. After a while, the stream of people became a trickle. Finally the platform was empty. Hachiko flicked his ears, listening for the sound of familiar footsteps. Train after train pulled in and out of the station. The night grew dark and chilly. When the final train steamed away and the lights went out, Hachiko returned to his home alone. He did not know that his dearest friend had suffered a stroke during a faculty meeting and had died that afternoon. Professor Ueno would never walk through the gate at Shibuyu station again.

It was the custom in Japan for a body to be placed out for viewing at home. There are several stories about what happened the night after Professor Ueno died. Some say that Hachiko never saw his master. Another report claimed that the dog, who had been left in the garden, broke into the house. He refused to leave his master and stayed close beside the body all night. According to another story, Hachiko found the room where Dr. Ueno's things were stored. He remained in the room, and he did not eat anything for three days.

Hachiko was confused. He walked to the station again and again looking for his dear friend. Eventually Professor Ueno's widow sold her home. She sent the grieving dog to live with relatives in Asakusa, in the eastern part of Tokyo. To Hachiko, the new place was not home. He ran away again and again to his master's home in Shibuya. Even though it was a distance of eight miles, he knew the way. When the new owners of Professor Ueno's home chased Hachiko away, he would go to the station to watch and wait.

Ueno's widow tried again. Thinking the countryside would be a good place for a dog, she sent the Akita to live with relatives on a farm in Setagaya. The new setting was even worse than the last. Hachiko was not used to country life. He annoyed neighboring farmers when he trampled through crops. He upset everyone

Grave of Professor Ueno and monument to Hachiko in the Aoyama Cemetery.

when he splashed through rice paddies. It became clear that
Hachiko would never adjust to new owners. Finally a man named
Kikusaburo Kobayashi offered to give the heartbroken dog a
home. Kobayashi had been Professor Ueno's gardener. The elderly
man had known Hachiko as a puppy, and he lived in Yoyogi
near Shibuya.

It was a fitting match. The gardener was patient and allowed the
dog to roam freely. Once again, Hachiko returned to the station day
after day to wait for his true master. The station director
remembered the Akita. At first he chased him away. When Hachiko
kept coming back, he let him stay. If it rained or the weather

turned bitterly cold, Hachiko would sometimes take shelter near the fireplace in the director's small cabin. The shopkeepers noticed that the dog kept his vigil without complaining. He never growled when a thoughtless traveler shoved him aside. He paid no attention when an unkind vendor tried to chase him away. The shopkeepers began to call him "Chuken Hachiko," or faithful dog Hachiko. They gave him water and small meals of sticky rice balls or little pieces of cooked meat.

The days turned into years. Spending much of his time on the street took a toll on the once beautiful dog. Battles with strays had left him with scars. One ear drooped down at an angle. In 1929, Hachiko developed a very bad case of mange. Tiny mites burrowed into his skin causing it to itch terribly. The beautiful pale fur became dull and fell out in patches. Over time the patches became raw and infected as Hachiko grew seriously ill. The weakened dog barely survived, but he did pull through. When he regained his strength, he returned to the station to the amazement of all who knew him.

It's a Fact: In Japanese Hachiko's name is written as 忠犬ハチ公 . The symbols mean "chuken hachiko," or faithful dog Hachiko.

One of Professor Ueno's students kept track of Hachiko's watchfulness. The young man visited Shibuyu several times over the years and noted that the dog was always at his post when the train arrived. The story of the loyal Akita was familiar to passengers who stopped in Shibuya, and they began to tell the amazing tale. In 1931, it came to the attention of Hirokichi Saito. The writer was a founding member of a club called NIPPO. The purpose of the club was to register and show true Japanese dogs. Saito had already written an article called, "The History on Preservation of Japanese Dogs." He had been looking for dogs that represented the traditional Akita with pointed ears and curled tails. He had also traveled to Odate and was disappointed when he found only three dogs that fit the description. After he returned to Tokyo, Saito heard the tale of the loyal Akita at the Shibuyu station. The writer decided to see for himself. He was thrilled when he did. Although Hachiko was quite bedraggled, he was indeed a perfect example of an Akita, a Royal Dog of Japan.

Saito wrote several articles about Hachiko. The first, "Faithful Dog Awaits Return of Master Dead for Seven Years," appeared on the 4th of October, 1932. It was printed in Japan's largest daily newspaper, the *Asahi Shinbun,* or *Asahi News.* The article caused quite a stir. Many people became interested in native dogs.

As news of the devoted Akita continued to spread, Japan was sinking into very hard times. The economy was doing poorly. People were working hard and making do with less. They began to take renewed pride in the basic elements of their society. Traits such as courage, determination, and loyalty became highly prized. Hachiko was an example of all of these traits. To encourage young people, the government created lessons about him for school textbooks. School children learned to love the dog. They wrote poems about him and sent him letters. One young boy in Yokohama wrote a letter to the stationmaster. The boy enclosed a little money in the envelope. He explained that it was pocket money that his parents had given him. He wanted it to be used to buy Hachiko a tasty treat to eat.

For most people in Japan at that time, owning a dog was not possible. Families couldn't afford to feed an animal or take care of it. Hachiko soon became the entire nation's pet. He was honored

It's a Fact: In Japanese folklore and children's stories, the dog is an important symbol of patience, loyalty, and goodness.

in many ways. Adults and children alike claimed that he was a symbol of everything a good Japanese citizen should be. Fans traveled to Shibuya station just to touch the Akita. Sometimes they brought food or filled his water bowl. Sometimes they just patted his head, stroked his fur, or offered kind words of encouragement. Many visitors thought that touching the dog would bring good luck and honor.

Hachiko took the attention in stride. He sat good-naturedly while children hugged him, nuzzled his neck, or even tugged on his ears or tail. When he needed a break, Hachiko simply slipped away to a quiet corner to rest. As each train pulled in, the dog's focus was always on the arrival gate. Every day he continued to wait at Shibuya station. He seemed to believe that Professor Ueno would come home.

By 1934, the Akita of Shibuyu had become a national symbol. On April 21 of that year, supporters placed a statue of Hachiko in front of the ticket gate of Shibuya station. Sculptor Ando Teru created the bronze tribute. It featured an engraved poem called "Lines to a loyal Dog." The unveiling of the statue was a popular event. It attracted a huge crowd. The grandchild of Professor Ueno was a special guest.

Unimpressed by the uproar, Hachiko also attended the celebration. He was the star of the show. Later in the year, a similar statue was placed near the entrance to the Odate station. It was not too far from the very cottage where Hachiko was born. At last, the years took a toll on the aging dog. He was stricken with a case of heartworm that made it difficult for him to breathe. On the early morning of March 8, 1935, Hachiko rested his weary head and breathed his last. His body was found near the very spot at the station where he had kept watch for ten years.

Hachiko's death was reported in the headlines of most major Japanese newspapers. The people of Japan were heartbroken. Even foreigners took the news with great sadness. The government declared a day of mourning. Faithful dog Hachiko was given full Buddhist rites, lasting forty-nine days. It was an honor no other dog had ever received. Many people chose to believe that when the devoted Akita closed his eyes for the last time, he opened them again in a different place. Perhaps it was a place where a smiling Professor Ueno held open the gate for his faithful dog. Perhaps they passed through that gate together.

The Akita's remains were treated with the greatest respect. His bones were buried in a corner of Professor Ueno's burial plot at Aoyama Cemetery. His coat was preserved. It became part of a figure of Hachiko on display at the Tokyo Museum of Art's National Science Museum.

Not long after Hachiko's death, Japan began to fight in World War II. In 1944, authorities collected the statues of the famous dog and melted them down to make ammunition. When the war was over, many people yearned to replace the statues that had stood for honor, loyalty, and trust. Times were still very hard, and there was little money for such a project. Once again Hachiko was in the headlines. Newspapers printed articles that retold the Akita's story. They suggested that there should be a new statue at the Shibuya station. Money poured in from countries around the world, including from Japan's wartime enemy, the United States. Ando Tekeshi, son of the original artist, made a bronze sculpture just like the one that had been destroyed. It was proudly placed at Shibuyu station during a ceremony on August 15, 1948.

The dog's bronze feet soon became bright and shiny from people rubbing them for luck. The simple figure still stands today in a corner of the station plaza. It has become a popular meeting spot. What better place to greet friends and family than near the image of the faithful and devoted Akita?

Bronze statue of Hachiko at Shibuya Station.

Hachiko's statue became a meeting place of choice for couples. It was so fashionable that it earned a new nickname, "Love-Knot Hachiko." Young men and women felt that if they declared their love in front of Hachiko, their love would last a lifetime.

Hachiko's legend has not dimmed over the years. On May 28, 1994, millions of Japanese people gathered around radios to hear the dog's voice. It seems that long before, someone had recorded him as he barked. Sadly, the long-playing record had been broken. There was no way to repair it at the time. At last, the Culture Broadcasting Network

Hachiko at the National Museum of Nature and Science, Japan.

(CBN) purchased the three broken pieces. Using laser techniques, workers repaired the recording. The radio show received plenty of publicity. Once again Hachiko's name became a household word. The audience waited through a stream of commercials to finally hear what had been silenced decades before. At last Hachiko spoke. "Wan-wan," he said. "Wan-wan" is the Japanese version of bow-wow.

Even now Hachiko is an important part of Japanese culture. Each year on April 8th hundreds of dog lovers gather for a ceremony at Shibuya station. They come together to honor the loyalty and devotion of the faithful Akita. Visitors leave food offerings at the statue to honor the spirit of loyalty. A beautiful mosaic of several playful Akitas adorns the wall of the station.

In 1964, a sculpture of an Akita family was placed near the Odate Station. A new Hachiko statue was added in 1988. There is also a small Hachiko shrine inside the station. Dog-loving tourists often take time to visit Hachiko's birthplace in Odate. Visitors may also include a trip to the Akita dog museum, where they can learn the history of the breed. Each year in spring an important Akita dog show is held during Golden Week in Keijo park. The park is small, but people come from every corner of Japan and even from other countries to show off their beautiful Akitas.

PART TWO
THE ROYAL DOGS OF JAPAN

The Akita is considered a natural treasure of Japan. The breed's ancestors were once a favorite of royalty, and so it became known as The Royal Dog. The history of the Akita is like a puzzle with some of the pieces missing. There are many clues, but there are many gaps too.

The forerunners of all ancient Japanese dogs may have come to the island nation by two different routes. Some may have come from China and Korea and entered Japan from the south. Others, like the ancestors of the Akita, probably started out in northern Europe. They crossed what is now Russia and moved into northern Japan. The ancient dogs probably traveled with hunters in search of food. The early people of Japan were hunter-gatherers. They lived in small "pit houses" which had straw-like roofs and dirt floors. Scientists have found evidence that these people kept dogs as household pets as long as three thousand years ago. Medium-sized dog skeletons have been uncovered in graves near such homes. Ancient art shows dogs with upright ears and curled tails. They look similar to modern Japanese dogs.

It's a Fact: The Japanese Spitz, the Japanese Chin, and the Japanese Terrier are not considered native Japanese dogs.

The early Japanese hunters were known as "matagi," and the ancestors of the Akita came to be known as "matagi dogs," or "matagi inu." Although they were smaller than the modern Akita, they

Akitas Hunting Yezo Bear, Akita-Inu Museum, Odate, Japan.

already had many of their descendents' traits. The mountainous regions of the area were often covered by snow during the winter, so the dogs regularly hunted in deep snow. They relied on their keen eyesight and excellent sense of smell. With great determination they tracked and cornered antelope, deer, boar, and even bears and monkeys, as well as smaller game. The hunters could then bring down the prey with a spear or arrow.

There are several breeds of native Japanese dogs including the Akita inu, Hokkaido inu (or Ainu), Kishu inu, Kai inu, Shikoku inu, and Shiba inu. Most of the breeds are named for the area where they developed. The Shiba inu is an exception. Its name means "little brushwood dog," and it is the smallest of the native breeds. The Akita is one of the largest of the native breeds.

The story of the Akita has taken some brutal turns. In the early 1300s, Takatoki Hojo was in power as a Regent in Japan. A ruthless man, he was a great fan of dog fighting as entertainment. His subjects offered fierce dogs as a way of paying taxes. Wealthy people often gave the Regent groups of fighting dogs as gifts. The dogs were fed better than most peasants. They ate meals of fish, duck, and other delicacies. They wore fitted silk coats decorated with raised designs woven with metallic threads. Takatoki had a few thousand of the dogs, and fights took place monthly for his amusement. The Regent and other nobles would watch the cruel events while sitting on silken cushions.

It's a Fact: The words "inu" and "ken" both mean "dog" in Japanese. Inu is actually the Japanese word for "breed."

The medium-sized dogs that the Regent admired often came from the Tohoku region of Japan. The area included the Akita Province. People living there knew that the dogs were not only excellent at hunting and fighting, but at guarding as well. By the 17th century, the area was well known for dogs of a specific size and character. Ancestors of the modern Akita, they were called the Regional dogs and were highly prized.

Common people were not allowed to own these early Akitas. Outside of the area where they were bred, Regional dogs were owned only by royalty and by the shoguns, military commanders who ruled under the emperor. As in the early days of the matagi, they used the dogs to track elk, antelope, wild boar, and bear. And not just any bear, but the fierce, eight-hundred pound Yezo bear. As the legend of the dogs' bravery and steadfast character spread, the shoguns collected them as living trophies. They even used special "dog" words to speak to and about the animals.

Some historians think that members of the warrior class could also interact with the dogs. The warriors, called "samurai," were respected and admired for their ability to fight. The courage and bravery of the Regional dogs inspired the samurai. The warriors studied the way the dogs fought.

The greatest possession a samurai had was his honor. If necessary, it was his duty to die with courage. There was a legend that if a warrior died without honor, he might have a chance to redeem himself. His spirit could be reborn in the body of an Akita. If he then died defending his master, he would reclaim his honor.

A samurai warrior.

Traditional Akita collar.

The daily care of the royal dogs from Akita was an important ritual. There were strict ceremonies for bathing and feeding. Each dog had a collar and lead that showed the rank and social standing of the owner.

In the mid-1600s, a shogun came to power who made life much better for the dogs. In fact, he is remembered as the Dog Shogun Tsunayoshi. This ruler cared very deeply for the lives of animals. He passed an important and powerful law against animal cruelty. Unkind acts directed at animals led to imprisonment. Since the law required that sick animals had to be treated, the first dog doctors were recognized. There were also special workers called the "Inu-metsuke." They kept track of the age, gender, and fur color of all dogs. Sadly, people were so afraid that they might be caught breaking the law that they dumped family dogs in the street to fend for themselves. The shogun passed new orders to build and feed the stray dogs. When Tsunayoshi died in 1709, the laws were all reversed, but by then there were thousands of street dogs.

The Dog Shogun.

By the end of the century, things went from bad to worse. Farmers' crops failed. Japan suffered through a famine that killed more than 7,000 people in the province of Akita alone. The terrible time was known as the Rabbit Year Starvation. Society started to fall apart. People were in great danger, and many families used a guard dog for protection. The Regional dog was perfect for the job. Like modern Akitas, it didn't bark unless there was danger. It could also be trained to herd and protect livestock. It wasn't long before people who lived in the town of Odate crossbred their dogs with larger foreign dogs such as Tibetan Mastiffs and Great Danes. The result was a larger, more aggressive dog that came to be known as the Odate dog. Not only was it a good guard dog, but also since dog fighting had become popular again, the Odate dog was a favorite in the ring.

A final blow came when Japan had an outbreak of the deadly disease called rabies. It was usually fatal to animals and could be passed from infected dogs to people. More than 3,000 cases were reported. Both sick and healthy dogs were killed to prevent the illness from spreading.

During the 1800s, particular families bred the dogs of Akita. The resulting animals became known by their color and family name, such as the White of Adachi, the Brindle of Benzousama, and the Black of Izumi.

At the dawn of the 20th century the tide turned in favor of the canines once more. In 1900, two Odate dogs were presented to the Emperor Taisho. He appreciated the breed for its strength of character and excellent temperament. The emperor declared that they should not belong just to royalty, but to all the people of Japan. The general population was very enthusiastic, and the popularity of the Odate dog grew.

Although dog fighting had become a large, well-organized business, it was finally outlawed in 1908. Instead of being known for their aggression and fighting skills, the Odate dogs were soon valued for their beauty and value as companions. They were very intelligent and had many more wonderful qualities. The Odate dog could be trained as a cattle herder, a seeing-eye dog, a sled dog, and even as a police dog. Although the dogs didn't particularly like water, their webbed feet made them good swimmers. Fisherman trained them to drive schools of fish toward their nets. Amazingly, the dogs who had once been champions in the fighting ring were excellent family pets. They were patient and so gentle with children that parents often used them as babysitters.

When two Odate dogs were shown at the Taisho Exposition of 1914, specialists began to take notice. It was clear that there had been a lot of crossbreeding. The experts realized that if the traditional Japanese breed was to survive, they must take action.

The Akita is a symbol of good health. People in Japan often send little Akita statues to new parents as a wish for a healthy baby. Similar figures are sent to wish a speedy recovery to someone who is sick.

Dr. Shozaburo Watase promoted a law that ensured the protection of native dogs. To do this he had to figure out what a traditional native dog would look like and how it would act. Would it be large? What color would it be? Dr. Watase traveled to Odate, but he found a wide variety of dogs, and no one could agree about which had the best traits. Scientists and breeders held meetings to discuss the issue. When no one could come up with a standard for the breed, many people lost interest. The Odate mayor, Shigeie Izumi, established a society to preserve the dog from the Akita area. The society was known as AKIHO, but at first it had no members. The mayor and a few other residents had a few excellent hunting dogs that had not been crossbred. It was then that the stories about Hachiko began to catch the attention of the public.

In July 1931, approximately nine Odate dogs were confirmed as perfect examples of a Japanese dog, and the breed was declared a natural monument. The name was then changed from Odate dog to Akita Inu, and the breed became very popular.

In 1932, a newspaper article brought Hachiko to the attention of the nation. Not only was he an excellent example of what an Akita should look like, he was an example of the way an Akita should behave. Hachiko became a symbol of all the wonderful traits of the dogs of Odate. The public began to take great pride in the native dogs.

Two years after Hachiko passed away, the famous American, Helen Keller, visited Japan. She had heard about the beloved Akita and wanted to own one for herself. The Japanese people adored Miss Keller and even called her a living saint. They were truly honored that she wanted to bring an Akita into her life. In August of 1937, a breeder brought Miss Keller a sweet male puppy named Kamikaze-Go. His nickname became Kami, and he shared her stateroom on the ship when she returned to the United States. The passengers tickled and petted the pup when he walked on deck. The journey took sixteen days, and by the time it was over, Helen Keller was devoted to the little Akita. Miss Keller's teacher, Ann Sullivan, had died the year before, and Miss Keller still sometimes cried about it. She said that when that happened, Kami would touch her knee with his paw or lick away her tears.

Helen Keller and her beloved Akita, circa 1938.

Helen Keller wrote about her precious pet, Kamikaze-Go in the *Akita Journal*. She noted, "If ever there was an angel in fur, it was Kamikaze. I know I shall never feel quite the same tenderness for any other pet. The Akita dog has all the qualities that appeal to me. He is gentle, companionable, and trusty."

Sadly, the young dog came down with a case of distemper and died before he reached the age of eight months. Miss Keller was heartbroken. When the breeder heard of the tragedy, he sent Kami's brother to America as a gift from the Japanese government. The pup's name was Kenzan-Go, which quickly became just Go-Go.

Go-Go and Miss Keller lived together in Connecticut for many years. She wrote that he was, "a splendid protector and companion, and a precious part of my daily life." She loved how he would tell her "with his nose, ear, and tail to play with him."

> It's a Fact: In 1947, after World War II, Miss Keller returned to Japan and gave her thanks for the joy and love that the Akita had brought to her life. She also called the breed a contribution toward peace.

World War II

Just when it seemed that the Akita had taken its rightful place in history, the breed was dealt another blow. Japan became involved in World War II. Because supplies of food were limited during the war, keeping and feeding a dog was not allowed. In fact, countless dogs were to be destroyed. To save them, some owners released their beloved dogs in the rugged mountains. Although many probably died, at least a few had a chance to survive by hunting.

Hundreds of dogs were killed and used as food. Their fur was saved to line clothing for the military. The only dogs that were permitted to live were the German Shepherds used as guard dogs by soldiers. Some Akita owners crossbred their dogs with German Shepherds hoping to save the line. They also called their dogs by German and American-sounding names, such as Carl and Mary, that were often given to German Shepherds.

When the war was over, there were only about twenty purebred Akitas in all of Japan. There were, however, a new group of dogs that had mixed Akita and German Shepherd blood. They were larger and some had different markings from the traditional Akita. This led to two types of dogs within the same breed. The Ichinoski line represents the Japanese Akita of today. These Akitas must have light markings on the face and the underside of the dog.

A dog of the Dewa line has a loosely curled tail and a black mask and black markings. American soldiers preferred the larger Dewa Akitas and brought many to the United States. Purists consider the lines as two different breeds. Others believe they are simply two types of Akita.

It's a Fact: Champion traditional Akitas are considered national art treasures in Japan. If the owner cannot care for them properly, the government will contribute to their support.

Champion American Akita: Devpoints CH TimberSky TopSecret Shiojiri.

The Akita Club of America was founded in 1956. In 1973, the Akita breed was accepted into the American Kennel Club's Working Group. The American Akita is heavier-boned and has a more shepherd-like snout than its counterpart in Japan. Still, they have similar long legs, erect ears, and the famous curled tail and thick coat. The American Akita is often called the Great Japanese Dog, but it is easy to tell that it is an Akita.

Although the standard modern Akita has a thick but fairly short coat, there is a rare long-haired variety of the breed. An Akita with such a coat is called a "Moku" and is named after a dog that was born in Akita Province around 1854. Moku-Go was a pinto-colored dog with unusually long fur. A legendary fighting dog, he lived in the Jououji Temple in Odate. According to local tales he was nearly three feet tall at the shoulder and strong enough for two children to ride on his back. Moku-Go was said to have the spirit of a true warrior and could fight three opponents at a time. Today, if both parents carry the gene for longer fur, a Moku puppy can be the result. Although it is usually considered a fault, some Akita fans love the softer, silkier fur of the Moku.

Among the most popular traits of the modern Akita are its intelligence and loyalty. Hachiko is a fine example of faithfulness. Akita enthusiasts also recount a very popular legend about another loyal dog named Shiro. It is said that sometime in the 1700s, a hunter was permitted to hunt on a shogun's land. The hunter was chasing after his prey one day when he strayed onto another noble's land. When he was captured, he realized that he did not have his permit with him. The guards tossed him into prison. His hunting dog, Shiro, an Odate dog, followed his master and tried to comfort him. The hunter sent Shiro to retrieve the hunting permit. The dog crossed the mountains alone, a trip of nearly ten miles. The hunter's wife had realized that her husband had left without the permit. When Shiro arrived she slipped it into his collar. Although he ran the distance as fast as he could, the dog did not make it back in time and the hunter was executed. Even so, the villagers of the town praised his loyalty. They built the Rouken Shrine, also known as the Shiro Temple, over the dog's grave. The shrine, which sits atop the mountain of Kuzuhara, is a popular destination for Akita fanciers from around the world. People gather annually on April 17th to honor Shiro.

Without a doubt, the history of the Royal Dog of Japan is a long, complex, and a colorful one! Several times over the centuries the beautiful dogs and their ancestors came close to being wiped out. Now their future seems secure as people learn about the many wonderful features of this incredible breed.

Photo by Suki Maha

The bond between Akita and owner is legendary.

PART THREE
THE AKITA TODAY

Ask an Akita owner to describe their dog and they will probably use words such as loyal, devoted, fun-loving, and even goofy. Still, the first thing most people notice about an adult American Akita is its size and appearance. The Akita is a big, heavy-boned dog. The average male is a little more than two feet tall at the shoulder. He can tip the scales at 100 pounds or more. Females are smaller and more slender.

The sturdily built Akita has a broad, short, bear-like head, medium-sized upright ears, and a fluffy tail that curls up and over its back. One of its most amazing physical traits is its beautiful plush coat. The breed was developed in a land known for deep winter snows, so the coat is thick, warm, and virtually waterproof. It's made up of two layers. The dense undercoat is soft and wooly. The outer coat is made up of fairly short coarse fur. The dog has no problem in cold climates, but he can adjust well to warmer areas too.

An American Akita comes in a wide range of colors or combinations of colors including white, cream, black, red, chocolate, silver-gray, brindle, and pinto. The dog may or may not have a black mask.

A healthy American Akita with a thick, luxurious coat.

Japanese Akitas are lighter-boned than their American cousins. Their coats come in white, red, and brindle colors only, and they do not have black masks.

All dogs are individuals, but like any breed, the Akita is known for a particular temperament and behavior. The typical Akita is dignified and reserved in manner. He carries himself with the noble bearing of his royal ancestors. His nature is to be devoted to his master and loyal to his family and friends. To those he loves he is affectionate and patient. When properly trained he can be gentle and caring with children and smaller pets. To bring out these wonderful traits an Akita should be treated with affection and given a little time to himself when he needs it.

An Akita takes a very close look at the family cat.

The breed is often aloof and reserved with strangers, but Akitas are always alert and watchful. Akitas are not generally aggressive towards people, but they are protective of their family. The dog is usually territorial about his home and fearless in the face of danger. He may respond with force if he sees someone as a threat. An intruder could certainly come to harm by threatening an Akita or his people. Because the Akita is strong and powerful, he should not be left alone around strangers, particularly unfamiliar children and small animals.

The Ideal Home for an Akita

Here are some tips to help prospective owners decide if an Akita is right for them.

- The Akita is a powerful dog best suited to an experienced dog owner.
- Children in the family will treat the puppy gently and with respect.
- Additional pets must be carefully socialized with the Akita puppy.
- Apartment dwellers must have access to a suitable area to exercise the puppy.
- Homeowners will need a fenced yard.
- The puppy will be obedience trained.
- The owner knows and accepts the costs of quality food, veterinary care, license fees.
- The owner is prepared to care for the dog for the rest of its life.

Akitas are independent and do not require constant attention. They are also curious, extremely intelligent, and energetic so they should have supervision in social situations. For example, a local dog park can be a real treat for an Akita, but the royal dog usually wants to be in charge of other dogs. An owner should keep an eye on his or her Akita to be certain that he is "playing nicely." Akitas don't need quite as much exercise as other large breeds. They are generally calm dogs and not known to bark a lot unless they have a good reason. That makes the breed a possible choice for big-dog-loving apartment dwellers. Still, the Akita is a working dog and may become bored and destructive if left alone for hours.

The ideal source for an Akita puppy is a responsible breeder. Such a puppy is most likely to be healthy, well adjusted, and better socialized. A potential owner who works with a breeder will be able to observe the parents, watch the puppy play with its siblings, and get a good idea about the young dog's individual

Akita puppy at eight weeks.

temperament. If for some reason the new owner still finds that he or she cannot keep the puppy, a responsible breeder will take it back or help place it in a new home.

What to Look for In a Breeder

- They offer one or two breeds only.
- They allow the buyer to meet the parents of the litter.
- They allow the buyer to observe the puppy at play.
- The premises are comfortable and clean with little or no odor.
- They guarantee their pups free of genetic diseases common in their breed.
- They offer references from previous puppy buyers.
- They will ask the buyer to fill out a questionnaire and/or provide references.
- They provide a contract that protects all parties.
- Breeder will provide directions for feeding.
- They check in with the new owner to see how the puppy is doing.

Responsible breeders usually offer show-quality and/or pet-quality dogs. Pet-quality puppies may not be ideal for the show ring, but they can be wonderful members of a loving family. Breeders generally sell pet puppies at a lower price and require that they be spayed or neutered.

Here are some important questions to ask before you buy a new Akita puppy.

- Have both of his parents been x-rayed for hip dysplasia and checked for eye diseases?
- Does the breeder provide a health record with worming/puppy shots/well puppy vet check?
- Are the parents registered with the OFA (Orthopedic Foundation for Animals)?
- Are the parents certified free of PRA (progressive retinal atrophy) and other eye diseases?

A great Akita is one that is well trained. To be a good canine citizen a dog must learn the rules early. It is very important for an Akita puppy to be socialized. The lessons begin as a puppy interacts with its mother and littermates. As the pup grows he learns the body language and signals used in canine communication.

Puppies must be taught to accept human interaction too. A young dog that is handled gently learns that human contact is pleasant and will become skilled at overcoming fear and stress. A well-adjusted dog is confident in a variety of situations. The more familiar a puppy is with his world, the more confident he will be. The earlier a new puppy meets family members, including household pets, the better. If a young Akita is introduced to a cat or bird in a comfortable atmosphere, he can learn to accept that pet as a friend.

Socializing a Puppy

- Introduce puppy to a range of people young and old.
- Expose puppy to strollers, wheelchairs, canes, walkers, grocery carts, luggage, skateboards, umbrellas, and any other tools and toys that people use.
- Familiarize puppy with street sights and sounds such as clanking trucks, motorcycles, joggers, and bicyclists.

It's a Fact: An Akita will guard his home and family naturally. It is not necessary to train the dog to do so. In fact, an Akita should not be given guard dog or protection training.

A properly trained Akita may get along well with other dogs.

Akitas don't respond well to tough training methods. They get bored easily and can resent being corrected. Although the Akita is devoted and truly wants to please his owner, he isn't a pushover. Some people claim that the breed can be stubborn, but training an Akita just takes patience and positive reinforcement. Countless Akitas have been obedience trained very successfully and have even passed the Canine Good Citizen Program from the American Kennel Club. An Akita will learn his lessons as long as the owner is consistent and lovingly firm.

Adopting a dog of any breed should be a lifelong commitment. It is the pet owner's responsibility to do the proper research to be certain that a new pet is well matched to the routine and personalities of the household. Rescue shelters across the country are filled with wonderful, loving Akitas who were not suited to the lifestyles of their owners.

Double-coated dogs, like Akitas, need regular grooming. He should be brushed at least once a week to promote clean, healthy skin and a glowing coat. Brushing removes loose hair that can cause itching. Two or three times a year the Akita sheds dramatically. This is called "blowing its coat." During these times, to avoid drifts of cast-off fur from gathering in every corner of the home, the dog must be brushed once or even twice daily. Regular bathing isn't as critical, and many Akitas are not too fond of getting their coat wet.

It's a Fact: In some ways an Akita may be almost catlike in its habits, including carefully cleaning its face after eating.

Bathing an Akita

- Use a gentle shampoo and coat conditioner designed for dogs.
- Use water that is comfortably warm, not hot.
- Start from the back of the dog, leaving his head and face for last.
- Do not get water or soap in the dog's eyes, ears, or mouth.
- Rinse very carefully. Leftover soap can irritate the skin.
- Conditioner helps to keep the coat soft.
- A blow-dryer can frighten some dogs. A large thirsty towel will usually do a fine job.

Everyday care is the first step in protecting an Akita, but like every breed of dog, they may have health issues. It is a good idea to read about illnesses that may affect Akitas before beginning the search for a furry family member.

It is important for a pet owner to be familiar with any symptoms that may signal health concerns. Good nutrition, exercise, and regular veterinary check-ups will help an Akita live a fit, happy life for as many as 12 or 15 years.

The Akita breed is often called "Ichiban," Japanese for "Number One." Without a doubt, the Akita is a magnificent friend with a heart of gold and the spirit of a samurai. Owning and training one is not always simple, but a responsible and loving pet owner will be rewarded with a lifetime of joy and affection from the royal dog of Japan.

Glossary

A.K.I.H.O.   Japanese society and club, which was created to protect Akitas.

Akita   Large, muscular Japanese dog; known as the royal dog of Japan.

American Kennel Club   The official organization for keeping track of types of dog breeds in America.

Breed   A type of dog. Akitas, Great Danes, Poodles, and Terriers are examples of breeds.

Breeder   The job of a person who raises a specific type of dog.

Brindle   The pattern of colors on a dog's fur; similar to the stripes on a tiger.

Canine   Another word for dog or like a dog.

Champion   A dog becomes a champion dog when it has been evaluated by judges at contests to be ideal for its breed.

Crossbreed   A combination of two different breeds, or types, of dog.

Distemper   Potentially fatal disease that affects some dogs.

Gene   Code of cells that determine what an animal (including humans) looks like.

Guard dog   A dog trained to protect its property. Rottweilers and Dobermans are examples of guard dogs.

Heartworm   Animal disease causing breathing difficulty and possibly death.

Hip dysplasia   Disease in dogs that can cause pain and difficulty walking.

Ichinoski (Itch-ee-no-skee)   Descendants of Akitas popular in Japan today.

Litter The full group of puppies that a dog gives birth to.

Mange Dog disease where small insects burrow in fur and cause itching and loss of fur.

Mask The change in colors on a dog's face around its nose, eyes, and mouth.

Moku (Mo-koo) An Akita with long hair.

Neutered A medical procedure done to male dogs so that they can't reproduce.

N.I.P.P.O. A club created to showcase and protect Japanese dogs.

Obedience training Teaching a dog to follow commands, like "Sit" and "Rollover."

Odate Large guard dog crossbred between an Akita and large foreign dogs.

OFA Orthopedic Foundation for Animals; a society that cares for the joints and muscles of dogs.

Pinto A color pattern that makes it look like patches on an animal's fur.

Positive reinforcement When an owner gives their dog a treat for doing something well, so the dog learns to continue the good behavior.

PRA Progressive retinal atrophy; a disease that affects a dog's vision.

Purebred When two dogs of the same breed have a puppy.

Rabies A disease that causes dogs to get mad and violent; can be fatal.

Rescue shelter A place that gives a home to dogs that have run away or gone missing until they are adopted.

Shed When a layer of fur falls off a dog so that the new layer can grow in.

Snout Front part of a dog's face, including its nose, mouth, and jaw.

Socialized When a dog is taught to be friendly around other dogs.

Spayed A medical procedure done to female dogs so that they can't have puppies.

Stray Dog that has run away from home or lives in the wild.

Temperament The nature and character of an animal.

Territorial A trait of an animal that means to protect its area.

Tibetan Mastiff Large dog originating from Tibet and Central China.

Traits Characteristics of a breed: "friendly," "loyal," "angry," "energetic" are all examples of traits.

Veterinarian A type of doctor who only treats animals. They help animals who are sick, injured, or dying.

Worming A pill or paste that dogs take to rid their bodies of harmful worms.